GOVERNMENT MAPS

Gareth Stevens
Publishing

Please visit our Web site www.garethstevens.com. For a free color catalog of all our high-quality books, call toll free 1-800-542-2595 or fax 1-877-542-2596.

Library of Congress Cataloging-in-Publication Data
Government Maps / Tim Cooke, editor.
        p. cm. -- (Understanding maps of our world)
    Includes index.
    ISBN 978-1-4339-3515-2 (library binding) -- ISBN 978-1-4339-3516-9 (pbk.)
    ISBN 978-1-4339-3517-6 (6-pack)
    1. Political geography--Maps. 2. Administrative and political divisions--Maps. I. Cooke, Tim.
G1046.F1M28 2010
912.024'35--dc22   2009039214

Published in 2010 by
Gareth Stevens Publishing
111 East 14th Street, Suite 349
New York, NY 10003

© 2010 The Brown Reference Group Ltd.

For Gareth Stevens Publishing:
Art Direction: Haley Harasymiw
Editorial Direction: Kerri O'Donnell

For The Brown Reference Group Ltd:
Editorial Director: Lindsey Lowe
Managing Editor: Tim Cooke
Children's Publisher: Anne O'Daly
Design Manager: David Poole
Designer: Simon Morse
Production Director: Alastair Gourlay
Picture Manager: Sophie Mortimer
Picture Researcher: Clare Newman
9 -10

Picture Credits:
Front Cover: Department of Defense: br; National Archives

Brown Reference Group: all artwork

Center for Topographic Information: 15; Central Intelligence Agency: 36, 37t; Corbis: Bettmann 11, 24; Department of Defense: 7, 26, 33b; DigitalVision: 4m, 4b, 42; iStock: cjp 30; Chris Crafter 12; Graham Heywood 35; Dave Long 38; Jupiter Images: Ablestock 5m, 8; Photos.com 21t; Stockxpert 5t; Library of Congress: 9, 14, 18/19, 25, 28; Lockheed Martin: 31; NASA: Landsat 40; National Atlas: 17; Robert Hunt Library: 27t, 27b; Shutterstock: Paul Drabot 33t; Vladislav Gurfinkel 4t; Henryk Sadure 44; Hector Garcia Serrano 43; Steven Wright 5b; United Nations: 38

Publisher's note to educators and parents: Our editors have carefully reviewed the Web sites that appear on p. 46 to ensure that they are suitable for students. Many Web sites change frequently, however, and we cannot guarantee that a site's future contents will continue to meet our high standards of quality and educational value. Be advised that students should be closely supervised whenever they access the Internet.

Manufactured in the United States of America
1 2 3 4 5 6 7 8 9   12 11 10

CPSIA compliance information: Batch #BRW0102GS: For further information contact Gareth Stevens, New York, New York at 1-800-542-2595.

Contents

The Changing Shape of the World

1400

This map shows the world known to Europeans in the fifteenth century: Europe and parts of Asia and Africa.

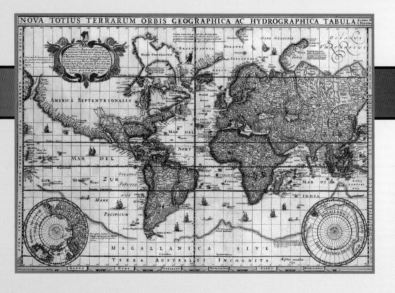

1700

1600

In this seventeenth-century map, only the interior of North America and the southern oceans remain empty.

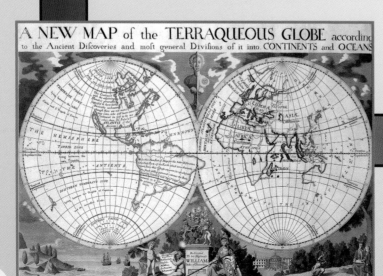

1800

This map reveals more information about Australia, but the northwest coast of North America and most of the Pacific Ocean remain unknown.

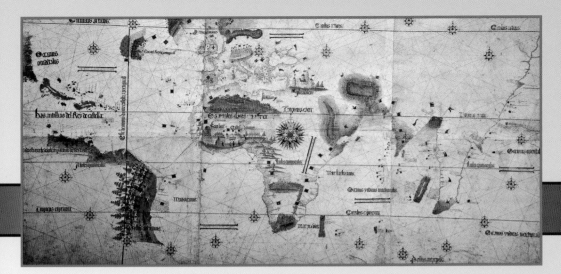

This sixteenth-century map fills in the coasts of Africa and India, the Caribbean islands, and parts of South America.

1500

In this sixteenth-century map, South America is only roughly shaped; the northwest coast of Australia has become part of the legendary "southern continent."

The first photographs of Earth from space were taken in the 1960s.

1900

This world map was drawn in 1875, when Europeans were at the height of claiming colonies in other lands.

5

Introduction

This is a volume from the set Understanding Maps of Our World. This book looks at how maps and mapping have been used by governments in peacetime and wartime.

UNDERSTANDING MAPS OF OUR WORLD IS AN eight-volume set that describes the history of cartography, discusses its importance in different cultures, and explains how it is done. Cartography is the technique of compiling information for, and then drawing, maps or charts. Each volume in the set examines a particular aspect of mapping and uses numerous artworks and photographs to help the reader understand the sometimes complex themes.

After all, cartography is both a science and an art. It has existed since before words were written down and today uses the most up-to-date computer technology and imaging systems. Advances in mapmaking through history have been closely involved with wider advances in science and technology. Studying maps demands some understanding of math and at the same time an appreciation of visual creativity. Such a subject is bound to get a little complex at times!

About This Book

Mapping is important for governments. It is one of the best ways to provide information about their peoples and lands, and to help governments plan for the future. Every nation realizes that having good maps of its own area is essential. This volume examines the history of official maps. It shows how governments organize mapping programs and what features they most commonly map (such as the landscape, their people, and the location of their natural resources). Maps also hold vital information for nations at war: Generals planning military campaigns use them, and so do soldiers on the battlefield. Maps can sometimes even be used for propaganda purposes.

Accurate maps can be a matter of life or death in wartime. Military needs were a major reason governments began mapping their countries and territories that they occupied.

Land Ownership

Maps are an important record of land ownership, establishing boundaries and other land rights, such as access to water.

MANY EARLY MAPS IN EUROPE WERE produced for rich and powerful people. These maps usually showed only the land belonging to the person who paid for it. In the mid-sixteenth century, however, a wealthy English landowner named Thomas Seckford paid the estate surveyor Christopher Saxton to survey and map every county in England. Saxton published his *Atlas of England and Wales* in 1579, which was the first atlas of the country.

European monarchies wanted maps of their own lands. They also paid for other countries to be mapped as a way of advertising their own importance. This is an elaborate seventeenth-century map of Portugal, drawn with an unusual western orientation. It was based on an original by Abraham Ortelius.

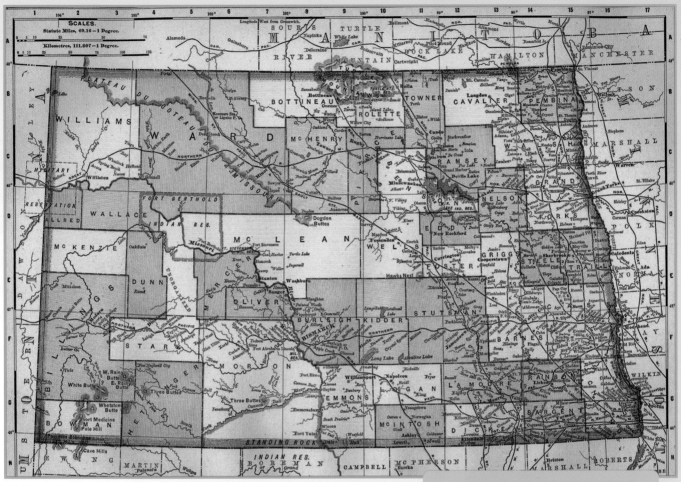

A 19th-century cadastral map of North Dakota, showing the straight lines of ranch divisions with the owners named within them. The state capital of Bismarck is in the south toward the center of the map.

Why Governments Need Maps

Governments need accurate maps for many different reasons. One of the most common motives is the need for accurate maps in times of war. The first national mapping agency, for example, was established in 1791 when Britain was at war with France. It was called the Ordnance Survey because the project was run by the Board of Ordnance, which was the government's defense department.

In other countries, governments realized the need for maps. After the American Revolutionary War ended in 1783, Thomas Jefferson began to organize the settlement and subdivision of new territory. This required cadastral maps. Cadastral maps register the ownership of land, and are essential to a government when it is setting taxes. The United States Public Land Survey System mapped more than 695 million square miles (1.8 billion sq km) to the west of the Appalachian Mountains.

Mapping Takeover

From the late seventeenth century on, governments began to organize mapmaking. New scientific methods were so expensive that usually only governments could afford them.

ONE WAY OF MAKING AN ACCURATE SURVEY USES A process called triangulation. One side of a triangle is measured accurately, and then trigonometry is used to calculate the lengths of the other two sides of the triangle. In this way a whole country can be accurately measured by dividing it into triangles. This takes time and requires money to pay for equipment and skilled surveying teams.

French Mapmakers

It was in France that triangulation and many other modern mapping techniques were first applied over a large area. Louis XIV was king of France from 1643 to 1715. His advisor Jean-Baptiste Colbert persuaded him that good maps were essential if he was to rule France effectively. Between 1675 and 1685 Colbert organized the first true surveying and mapping of France by the Académie des Sciences. Much of this was done using triangulation.

In 1684 a new map was produced showing the older outline of the French coast along with the new outline drawn by more scientific methods. Louis XIV is reported to have been very unhappy with the new map because it showed France to be smaller than

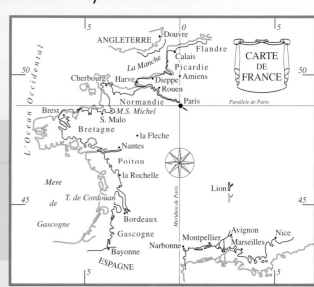

The map that made Louis XIV unhappy. It shows the old coastline and the newly drawn coastline, which made France smaller. The map is part of the *Carte de France Corrigée*, or "Corrected Map of France."

previously thought! He complained that his cartographers had lost him more land than any general—meaning that even wartime losses of territory could never be as big as the apparent loss of territory indicated by the new map. No land had been actually lost, of course; the older maps were simply wrong.

Major contributions to the early mapping of France were made by the Cassini family. César-François Cassini (1714–1784), the third generation of the Cassini family to work for the French monarchy, was a French astronomer and cartographer who directed the work on a map of the whole of France.

It was commissioned and paid for by the next king of France, Louis XV. Surveying began in 1747, but its completion was delayed by the French Revolution of 1789. The revolutionary government that overthrew the French monarchy eventually published the map in 1815 with the title *Carte Géométrique de la France* (Geometric Map of France). It was the first map of an entire country drawn according to modern mapping principles.

National Agencies

Governments around the world have set up national mapping agencies. The job of these agencies is to produce maps of their country.

THE SETTING UP OF NATIONAL AGENCIES HAPPENED at different times over a long period. Most countries of the world had no government mapping agency until after World War II (1939–45). Today, almost every country has its own national mapping agency. In some countries their main task is to complete the national map; in others it is to update existing maps.

In the early nineteenth century, very few of the topographic maps produced by national mapping agencies were sold to the general public. They were seen as official military documents. This view is still held by national mapping agencies in some countries.

The Ordnance Survey

The Ordnance Survey started to produce detailed maps of the south coast of Britain in the early nineteenth century so that

An Ordnance Survey Benchmark. When surveying an area, workers would cut one of these benchmarks into the stonework of a nearby building to mark a specific elevation. They would then use it as a reference point for their measurements. Benchmarks can be found all over Britain.

This modern map of the city of Edinburgh, Scotland, is drawn to a scale of 1:50,000. Red roads are main routes, yellow roads are fewer than 13 feet (4 m) wide. Numbers in red boxes show national cycle routes.

defenses could be strengthened against the French and army exercises could be carried out. The Ordnance Survey has been a wholly civilian organization since 1983. It produces more than a thousand different recreation and leisure maps a year. These maps come in many different scales and levels of detail, each suited to a different purpose. Billions of dollars worth of economic activity depends on its maps in some way, from building firms to haulage companies. Its importance to the British government lies in the information it supplies to help make decisions about the country's infrastructure. Where should industries be sited? What routes should new railroads take?

North American Agencies

The United States Geological Survey (USGS) produces maps for the government, for publishers, and for the general public. The U.S. Public Land Survey—set up in 1785 to help people register land claims— originally carried out this task. The USGS was established in 1879 to survey and map the new lands to the west of the original colonies. As its name suggests, it also mapped mineral and farming resources. High-quality topographic maps of the landscape helped in dividing up the land for incoming farmers and settlers. Mapping was also useful for constructing roads and railroads into the interior. Only in 1925 did the USGS start producing a topographical map of the entire United States. The job was not finished until 1990. The work of the USGS has now expanded into many other areas.

A map of Philadelphia produced in 1898 by the USGS. The map shows the street layout and low-lying marshy areas in the southwest but does not show height or the relief of the land.

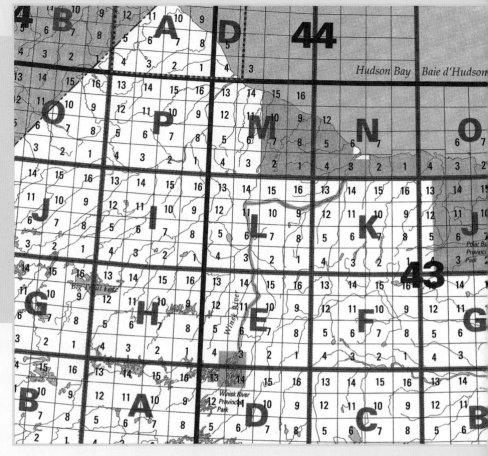

A Canadian map. Like many mapping organizations, the Center for Topographic Information uses a grid system to divide up the country, with each square identified by a letter or number. People can get larger scale maps of any area by referring to the grid letters and numbers. The modern Ordnance Survey map on page 13 also has a grid system to help the reader find places or features.

In Canada, the Center for Topographic Information produces maps of the country. The first maps were drawn by the Geological Survey of Canada, which was set up in 1841 to find and map mineral resources such as coal, gold, and iron ore.

War Improves Mapping Techniques

The biggest change in the work of national mapping agencies throughout the world happened in the twentieth century after World War II. A report produced by the U.S. Air Force in 1940 stated that less than 10 percent of the world was mapped in enough detail even for simple pilot charts. During the war it became clear that making maps from aerial photographs was a quick and accurate way of creating map coverage over a large area.

In peacetime, national mapping agencies adopted the techniques of photogrammetry (making measurements from photographs) to improve and complete national mapping. In addition, large areas of the developing world were mapped using photogrammetric methods. Maps were produced using aerial photographs taken of vast areas of Africa, Southeast Asia, the Caribbean, and the Middle East.

National Atlases

Many governments publish books that explain the physical and human geography of their country. They are called national atlases.

In 1970, the first national atlas of the United States was published. It consisted of a 400-page book of maps that gave information about the human and physical geography of the United States. It cost over $100 and so was usually found only in the libraries of schools and colleges.

The information in the book was presented in the form of thematic maps, graphs, and tables. The atlas contained sections on volcanoes, soils, and rivers, as well as human information such as crime patterns, population distribution, and patterns of disease. The information was gathered from all of the U.S. government's agencies, including the Census Bureau, the Department of the Interior, the Department of Agriculture, as well as the USGS.

Such books cover a broad range of topics, but are unable to examine them in the level of detail or specialization that many people need. In 1997, the USGS developed a new national atlas. This new atlas was placed online at www.nationalatlas.gov. As the technology used to display maps online has improved, the tools available to online users have become more comprehensive. The current site allows users to build their own maps from thousands of different data sets. They can also compare different phenomena—instantly creating a map that compares butterfly populations with agricultural pesticide use, for example.

Other National Atlases

More than 80 countries of the world now have national atlases, including Vietnam, Taiwan, Peru, El Salvador, and Tanzania. Some of these nations have produced atlases not just to show information about their country and its boundaries but also as symbols of independence after being ruled as a colony by a foreign power. Surprisingly few European countries have national atlases produced by national agencies.

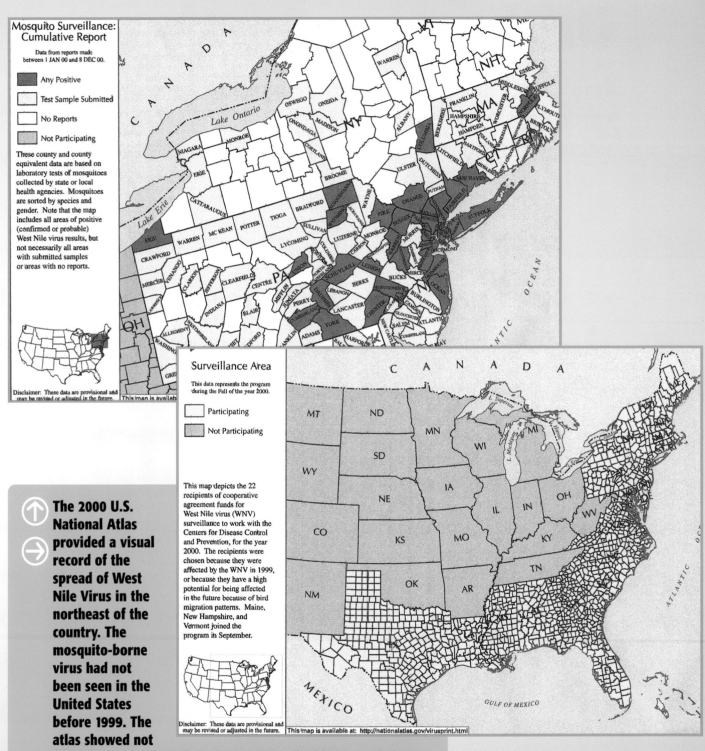

Mosquito Surveillance: Cumulative Report

Data from reports made between 1 JAN 00 and 8 DEC 00.

- Any Positive
- Test Sample Submitted
- No Reports
- Not Participating

These county and county equivalent data are based on laboratory tests of mosquitoes collected by state or local health agencies. Mosquitoes are sorted by species and gender. Note that the map includes all areas of positive (confirmed or probable) West Nile virus results, but not necessarily all areas with submitted samples or areas with no reports.

Disclaimer: These data are provisional and may be revised or adjusted in the future. This map is available

Surveillance Area

This data represents the program during the Fall of the year 2000.

- Participating
- Not Participating

This map depicts the 22 recipients of cooperative agreement funds for West Nile virus (WNV) surveillance to work with the Centers for Disease Control and Prevention, for the year 2000. The recipients were chosen because they were affected by the WNV in 1999, or because they have a high potential for being affected in the future because of bird migration patterns. Maine, New Hampshire, and Vermont joined the program in September.

Disclaimer: These data are provisional and may be revised or adjusted in the future. This map is available at: http://nationalatlas.gov/virusprint.html

The 2000 U.S. National Atlas provided a visual record of the spread of West Nile Virus in the northeast of the country. The mosquito-borne virus had not been seen in the United States before 1999. The atlas showed not just where tests for infected mosquitoes had been carried out and where they were positive, but also vast areas in the south of the country where testing was going to take place (see map, right). The problem is that the disease is carried by birds that have been bitten by infected mosquitoes. These birds then migrate south in the winter, taking the disease with them.

Under the Earth

Governments need maps of the minerals in the ground, which are a vital source of a nation's wealth. Until the nineteenth century, finding minerals was a matter of luck.

A PERSON WHO STUDIES ROCKS IS CALLED A GEOLOGIST. Geologists find out about rocks by noting where they appear on the surface (outcrops) and by examining mine shafts and quarries. Often they dig trenches, and they also drill through the surface. For geologists, maps are an important tool. For example, by plotting the distribution of different rock types on a map they can spot patterns that allow them to predict the location of other rock formations and mineral deposits.

More advanced techniques, such as seismic surveys, have allowed geologists to see further below the surface. In seismic surveys small explosive charges are detonated just below the ground. The shock waves from these explosions are then measured as they pass through and eventually reflect off underground features. Because these waves travel at different speeds through different rocks, geologists can map the underground features without digging or drilling. As a result, geological maps have to be able to record many different layers that extend far below the land.

Geological maps have many important applications. For example, an oil well can be as deep as 25,000 feet (7,600 m). This is too deep to see on a seismic survey. To find these oil deposits, geologists must examine maps for patterns of favorable rocks such as sandstones and siltstones.

The history of Australia is an example of just how important such discoveries can be. In 1946, the Bureau of Mineral Resources, Geology and Geophysics (BMR) was founded. It took about 20 years for surveyors to map the entire country. Massive mineral resources were found and exploited to transform Australia into a rich industrial nation.

A CROSS SECTION

William Smith (1769–1839)

The Australian geological surveyors, and geologists throughout the world, were following the lead of one brilliant mapmaker. The first nationwide geological map was of England and Wales, produced by William Smith in 1815. It was of economic importance because it helped locate the coalfields that provided the energy for Britain's industries.

   In most other countries, most of the geological mapping was done by government organizations. Smith's map, however, was a private project. It took him more than 15 years of field research and observation to produce his remarkable map.

This geological map from the 1860s uses different colors to show different rocks, like granite and coal. Such maps meant that people could predict where oil, coal, and gold might lie.

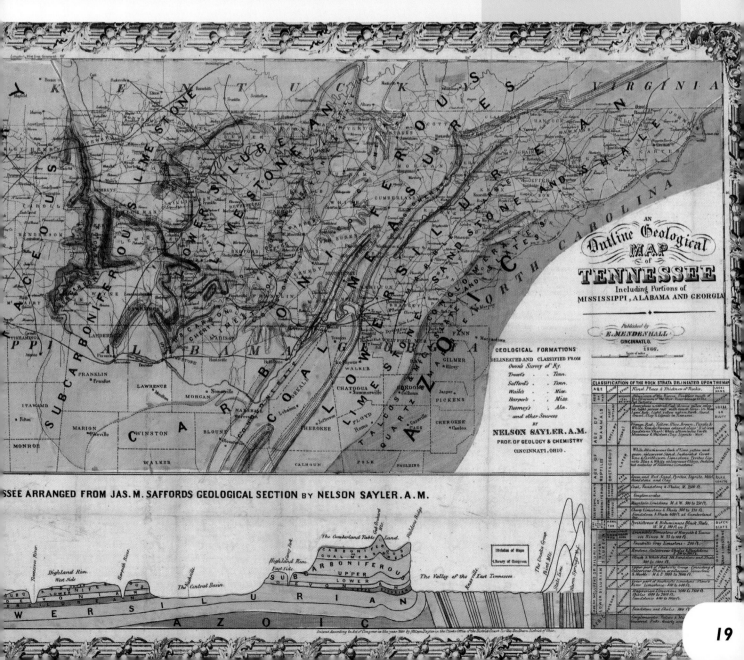

Mapping Population

Governments need to know about the people they govern. If they know their country's economic and social conditions then they can coordinate services and plan for the future.

GOVERNMENTS FIND THIS INFORMATION THROUGH A census. This is a count of how many people there are in a country and what those people are like. The census data can be used to create maps that show information, such as the distribution of people from different income levels, ethnic backgrounds, and levels of education.

The first census in the United States took place in 1790. A census has taken place every 10 years since then. Each time the number of people and the amount of information collected has increased.

The 2000 census was the largest ever. Most people filled out a form, which was sent to them by mail, but in remote places census enumerators visited people in their homes. Computers then analyzed the data. From the information the Census Bureau can produce maps showing details about people throughout the country. This is called the Tiger Mapping Service, and through the Internet anyone can gain access to this detailed information.

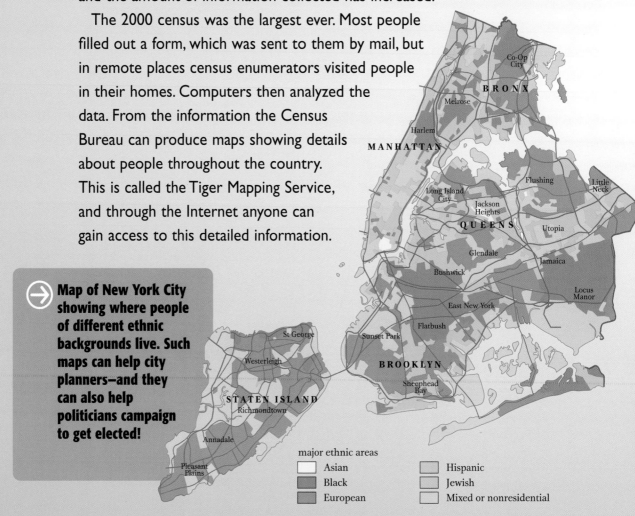

→ **Map of New York City showing where people of different ethnic backgrounds live. Such maps can help city planners—and they can also help politicians campaign to get elected!**

major ethnic areas

☐ Asian	☐ Hispanic
☐ Black	☐ Jewish
☐ European	☐ Mixed or nonresidential

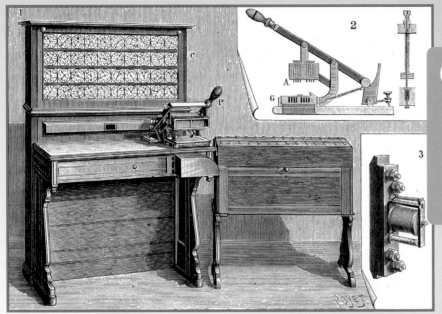

Diagram of the Hollerith Tabulator, which used holes punched into cards as a way of processing the data collected in the 1890 U.S. Census. It meant that the census results were organized in record time.

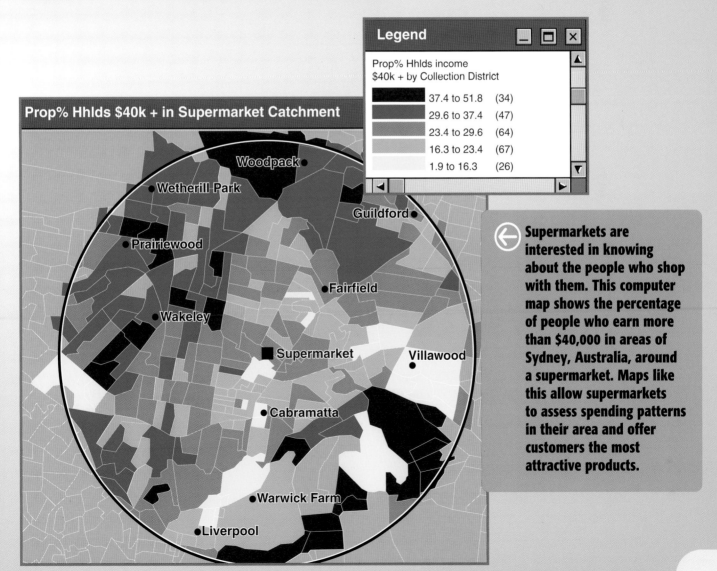

Prop% Hhlds $40k + in Supermarket Catchment

Legend

Prop% Hhlds income
$40k + by Collection District

■	37.4 to 51.8	(34)
■	29.6 to 37.4	(47)
■	23.4 to 29.6	(64)
■	16.3 to 23.4	(67)
■	1.9 to 16.3	(26)

Woodpack
Wetherill Park
Guildford
Prairiewood
Fairfield
Wakeley
■ Supermarket   Villawood
Cabramatta
Warwick Farm
Liverpool

Supermarkets are interested in knowing about the people who shop with them. This computer map shows the percentage of people who earn more than $40,000 in areas of Sydney, Australia, around a supermarket. Maps like this allow supermarkets to assess spending patterns in their area and offer customers the most attractive products.

Elections and Maps

A democracy is a form of government in which all of the adult people in a country have the right to vote in elections to decide who is to govern them.

IN A DEMOCRACY, THE COUNTRY IS USUALLY divided into electoral districts. During elections, the people of each district vote to decide who will represent them in government. These districts can be large (entire states) or small (neighborhoods) depending on what level of government the district is electing a representative for.

The results of the U.S. presidential election in 2000. The vote in Florida was very close and led to legal challenges to President Bush's overall victory.

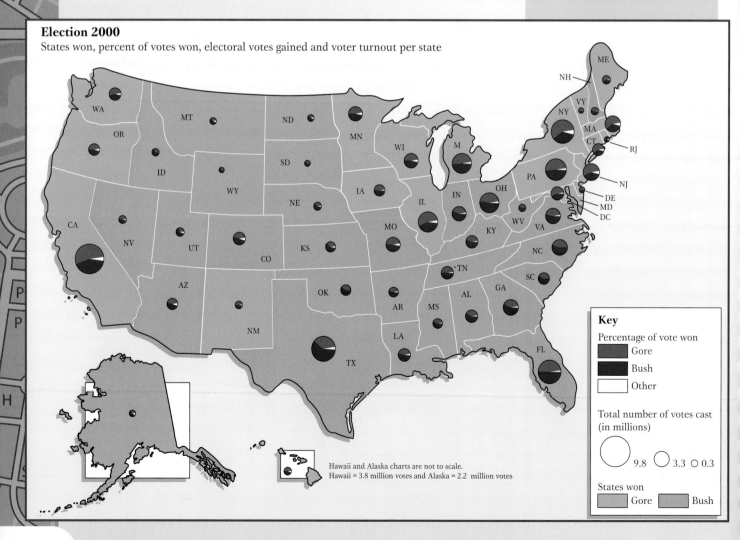

Election 2000
States won, percent of votes won, electoral votes gained and voter turnout per state

Hawaii and Alaska charts are not to scale.
Hawaii = 3.8 million votes and Alaska = 2.2 million votes

Key

Percentage of vote won
- Gore
- Bush
- Other

Total number of votes cast (in millions)
9.8   3.3   0.3

States won
- Gore
- Bush

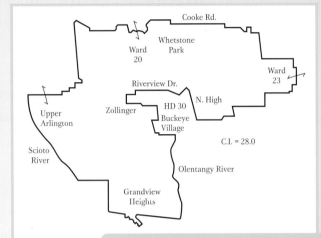

A cartoon of Governor Gerry's drawing of district boundaries, showing them as a kind of monster. The trick in gerrymandering was to make sure that opposing voters were all lumped together in one district. They would get only one vote. Neighboring (pro-Gerry) districts with fewer people in them each got a vote.

A "misshapen" electoral district in Franklin County, Ohio. The "hole" in the middle is an area of student housing for the Ohio State University. The students would tend to be Democratic voters, while the voters inside this district are predominantly Republicans.

At the national level, people in the United States not only vote for a president but also for someone to represent them in the House of Representatives and the Senate. Each state is divided into districts, and here too elections take place. Districts elect representatives to a wide range of roles within state and local governments. None of these electoral processes are possible without accurate maps.

Maps also play an important part in the television coverage of elections in all countries. TV studios use graphics of all kinds to show the results as they come in and the patterns of voting that are emerging. Similar maps are found in newspapers the next day.

Using Maps to Cheat

People in certain areas of a country tend to favor certain political parties. When such differences in voting patterns and preferences become known, some politicians move the boundaries between electoral districts in order to gain an advantage. Redrawing electoral districts to give one political party an unfair advantage is called *gerrymandering*. The name comes from Massachusetts governor Elbridge Gerry (1744–1814), who redrew the electoral boundaries of his state so drastically that his opponents said it looked like a giant salamander.

Maps and War

It almost seems as if war could not take place without maps, or at least not a modern war. Maps are essential to armies, navies, and air forces.

MILITARY FORCES NEED TO KNOW WHERE THEY ARE AND where the enemy is. They need maps to help them prepare attacks and defend themselves. The capture of an enemy's map gives an army a great tactical advantage.

The importance of maps in wartime can be seen by the fact that more than 34 million maps of the Western Front in France and Belgium were produced by the British, French, and American Allies during World War I (1914–18). Almost as many were produced by the Germans and other Central Powers.

During World War II (1939–45) British leader Winston Churchill used an underground bunker as his center of operations in London. The bunker was known as the Cabinet War Rooms, and in them was a place called the Map Room. It was here that, using maps hanging on the walls, battles were planned, and the progress of the war was monitored. They included maps of the Atlantic Ocean, the position of warships in the seas around the U.K., and maps showing the progress of American forces as they invaded island after island in the Pacific.

→ **Union General Quincy Gillmore studies a huge map of Charleston during the Civil War. Gillmore's Union troops were beseiging the city, which was being held by Confederate soldiers in 1863.**

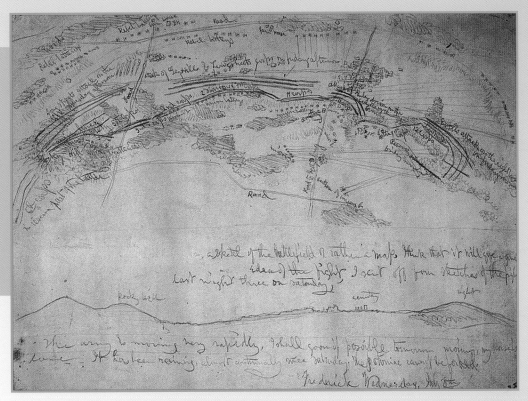

Thousands of these trench maps were produced during World War I. This one was used in an attack at Meuse-Argonne (above) by the American Army 1st Division on October 9, 1918. It shows the objectives for the attack.

More than 2,000 years before World War II the lack of a map probably stopped the conquest of India by the Greek commander Alexander the Great. Having conquered the huge Persian Empire and entered India, his weary army would go no further and mutinied. They simply did not know what lay ahead of them, and—despite the surveyors who accompanied him into Asia—neither did Alexander. Military history is full of moments when maps, and the interpretation of maps, made a huge difference.

Deadly Mapping Errors

Wartime maps have to be accurate, and those who use them must know how to read them. Mistakes have frequently been made in wartime that have resulted in the loss of lives of both soldiers and civilians. Artillery has hit and killed friendly troops either because the map was wrongly drawn, coordinates were wrongly given or understood, or the map was out of date.

Some map-reading mistakes have cost an entire war. Distances can look much shorter on a map than they are in reality. Converting a circular globe into a flat map also distorts distances.

A U.S. soldier entering map coordinates into the targeting system on a multiple-launch rocket system.

Maps misled German military commanders during the World War II. Their plans for the invasion of Russia relied on the fast movement of men and munitions. After the invasion began, German commanders discovered that most of the "roads" marked on the map were just dirt tracks. In the winter these dirt tracks became muddy and unusable, leaving many frontline troops stranded with little ammunition, no food, and no reinforcements.

Mapping the Seabed

It was not the needs and desires of geologists or marine scientists that led to the mapping of the ocean beds. It was those of the military. Some navies have nuclear-powered submarines that carry inter-continental ballistic missiles (ICBMs) with nuclear warheads. In the event of war these submarines would need to hide from enemy hunter-killer submarines. The need to find areas of the seabed on which to hide a nuclear submarine (and where to look for them) resulted in the mapping of the Atlantic and Arctic Ocean seabeds. This led to important discoveries about the movement of the Earth's crust (plate tectonics).

Maps from Spies

On page 10 we saw that Louis XIV arranged for maps to be drawn of the French coastline and that he was not happy with the results. He also had maps drawn of fortresses around the borders and coasts of France. In addition, using spies, he had maps made of forts in other countries.

Security was very lax in the French king's court. After the maps were created, copies of them were made. In 1683 the English ambassador in France contacted the English king Charles II and told him that he could get copies of the maps of French fortifications. The ambassador passed them on to Charles. They showed him more modern methods of building forts and castles.

More recently, many maps of different areas of the world have been prepared by the Central Intelligence Agency (CIA) for use by the U.S. military. They were made with modern methods of spying, which include reconnaissance aircraft flying very high over enemy territory and images from satellites. These maps provide accurate information about parts of the world that is not normally available.

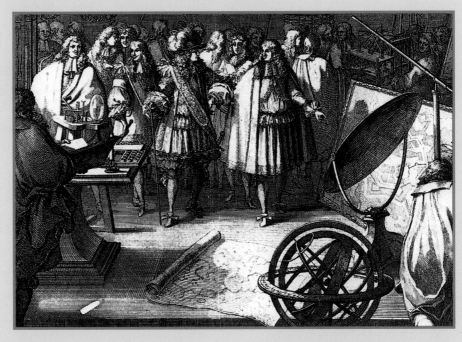

Maps and a celestial globe are featured in this engraving of Louis XIV, king of France, visiting the Academy of Sciences. The academy had been set up by him to study such topics as math and chemistry—but not espionage!

FISHBEDS WITH MISSILES UNDER WINGS

A photograph taken from a U.S. spy plane during the 1962 Cuban Missile Crisis. Aerial photos like these are often used to make maps.

27

Propaganda Maps

Propaganda is information presented in a way that encourages a community to adopt a particular viewpoint. It often involves telling lies or distorting the truth.

PROPAGANDA IS USUALLY DELIVERED THROUGH THE written word, speeches, or images. Maps can also be a very effective way of conveying a message and altering a person's opinion. Because maps are based on measurements of the world, they appear to tell the truth. People tend to trust a map.

Using maps as propaganda is not new. Some of the earliest maps were designed not just to record land ownership but also to make the person who commissioned it look important and influential.

In 1718, the French mapmaker Guillaume Delisle produced a map called *La Carte de la Louisiane et du Cours du Mississippi* (Map of Louisiana and the Course of the Mississippi River). He was paid by the French king for the work. On the map, "La Louisiane" is placed in broad letters across the entire

A map of British colonies in Newfoundland and the east coast of Canada. Like other British maps of the time, the map shows only the parts of the continent that the British controled, leaving out areas controled by France or Spain.

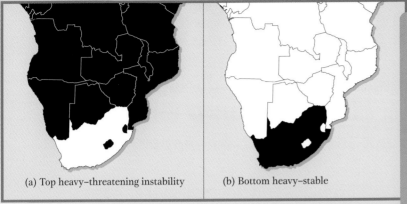

(a) Top heavy–threatening instability
(b) Bottom heavy–stable

Nothing is different on these two maps except the shading. But map (a) seems to be "unstable," the "weight" of countries presses on South Africa. Map (b) seems less threatening. Even something as simple as shading or color can change the way the map reader interprets a map. Although they may look like scientific facts, maps can argue a point of view, which means they can be used as propaganda.

Louisiana basin, and the English colonies are squeezed into a small area on the eastern coast. This map was a form of propaganda. It claimed a huge area of land for France to the west of the Appalachians.

It quickly provoked a response from the British. In 1720, Hermann Moll, a German map publisher working in London, produced *This Map of North America According to ye Newest and most Exact Observations*. On this map the British colonies stretch from the Carolinas to Newfoundland, and the ocean off the eastern seaboard is marked as "Sea of the British Empire." Several more maps were created by the French and the British in the following decades; each was a piece of propaganda. Neither the French nor the British actually controlled the vast tracts of land claimed at the time the maps were made.

A German propaganda map from the 1930s, "A SMALL STATE THREATENS GERMANY." Bomber aircraft from Czechoslovakia can apparently reach all of Germany. But the Czechs had no bomber aircraft!

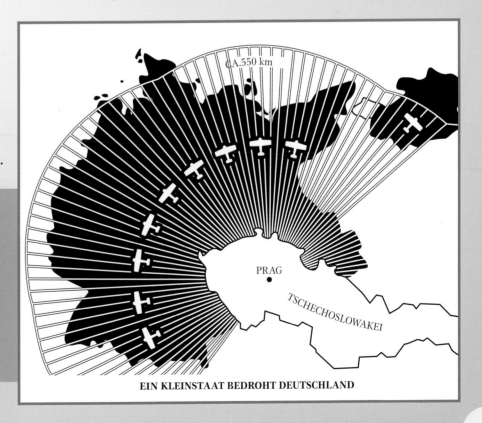

CA.550 km

PRAG

TSCHECHOSLOWAKEI

EIN KLEINSTAAT BEDROHT DEUTSCHLAND

Mapping the Enemy

Up-to-date, accurate maps are essential during a war, but drawing maps of an enemy's territory is very difficult. The enemy is not too eager to be mapped!

DURING WORLD WAR 1 (1914–18), TRENCH MAPS WERE BASED on pre-war French maps that were updated in several ways. Maps of areas behind enemy lines were often drawn from observation balloons and aircraft. Soldiers used to go on trench raids at night across no-man's land. The aim was to capture prisoners who were then interrogated for information. In some cases the prisoners had maps that showed where troops were located. While out on these raids the soldiers also drew sketch maps of the enemy trenches.

During World War II (1939–45), the maps used by the military were often based on very old tourist maps produced by commercial map-publishing firms.

In both world wars, reconnaissance aircraft flew over enemy territory taking photographs of the land below. During World War II, aircraft such as the Spitfire, P-51 Mustang, and Mosquito flew at both high and low altitude over Nazi-occupied Europe. They took photographs

→ During World War II, thousands of reconnaissance missions were flown by both sides. Navigators like this man were required to observe and chart the location of the enemy, as well as navigate their aircraft safely home.

that were used to locate enemy troops and buildings of importance, such as armament factories. The photographs these planes took were also used as the basis for accurate, up-to-date maps. The invasion beaches in Normandy in 1944 were mapped using aerial photographs and collections of old holiday photographs.

Flights of this kind do not take place only in wartime. The Germans flew civil airliners over Britain in the 1930s before World War II in order to take photographs. At the same time, the Germans were buying Ordnance Survey maps of the country. Although military information was deliberately missing from these maps, the Germans used their aerial photographs to alter and update the maps.

The SR-71 was a U.S. Air Force reconnaissance plane that flew at a height of 15 miles (24 km) and at 2,220 miles (3,550 km) per hour! It replaced the U-2 on dangerous missions because it was so fast that no missile or fighter plane could catch it.

Misleading Maps

Using the enemy's maps can be misleading. Not only are important features such as airports often missing, but also the enemy can deliberately put things in the wrong place. During the 1930s, and especially during the Cold War, Soviet mapmakers deliberately put information such as towns, rivers, hills, and coastlines in the wrong place on maps and atlases sold to the public.

In order to make more accurate maps, reconnaissance flights often took place during the Cold War. In 1962, an American U-2 aircraft flown by a pilot named Gary Powers was shot down over the Soviet Union. It was taking photographs that could have been used to map the land.

In the last three decades, satellites have reduced the need for reconnaissance flights. They orbit the Earth and can take very detailed photographs of the land below. The maps drawn from them can be produced very quickly.

The Three Cs

For any war to be won, a military leader must be able to command and control his troops. To do this, he must be able to communicate with them.

THESE BASIC REQUIREMENTS ARE STILL IMPORTANT, AND ALL of them require accurate and up-to-date information about the land, weather, and the position of different units.

Military Mapmakers

The job of producing maps for the U.S. military is in the hands of the National Imagery and Mapping Agency (NIMA), which was set up in 1996. It uses information from satellites, aircraft, and other sources to produce up-to-date and accurate images, intelligence, and geospatial information in the form of maps. NIMA produces maps for evasion and the location of targets for cruise missiles and bomber aircraft. NIMA can also use a computer to display a three-dimensional view of an area of land showing the shape of the Earth. Soldiers can sit at a computer and see a 3-D image of any place in the world.

These high-resolution radar maps are used to program cruise missiles such as the Tomahawk. This missile guides itself to its target following a

Eye in the Sky

Those countries that are members of the North Atlantic Treaty Organization (NATO), such as the U.S., Canada, and the U.K., use aircraft like the Boeing A-3 Sentry to get information. This airplane—also known as AWACS (Airborne Warning and Control System)—has a huge radar dome on its back, which is able to look down on a large area and spot movement of enemy aircraft, ships, and vehicles.

These movements are shown on radar displays that resemble video-game screens. Large crews of radar operators use the radar to detect the speed and positions of targets, which are overlaid onto topographic maps showing roads, towns, rivers, hills, and other prominent features. They use these electronic maps to control and direct their own forces against the enemy and to spot any attacks. The high-resolution radar on these aircraft can produce three-dimensional images that show the shape of the land in great detail. Satellites can also produce detailed maps of the surface of the Earth, and from them accurate topographical maps can be made.

As a result, producing up-to-date maps of any area of the world can be done quickly and accurately without having to use old, out-of-date maps or spies on the ground.

map of its intended route that has been made using radar images from satellites and aircraft. The map is programmed into the Tomahawk's guidance system before launch. On its way to the target it uses its own radar to check the route it is following against the route that has been programmed in. It also checks on its position using a satellite global positioning system (GPS) in its guidance system. During the Gulf War, this missile was used on targets in Serbia and Iraq. Since then, it has been used on targets in Afghanistan.

Pilotless aircraft called UAVs (Unmanned Aerial Vehicles) can fly over a battlefield and gather information for making maps. These UAVs avoid having a valuable aircraft and its even more valuable human crew shot down and lost. Some models of reconnaissance drone are capable of performing mapping missions autonomously—once the mission has been planned they require the operator only for takeoff and landing.

The RQ-4 Global Hawk is an unmanned aerial vehicle operated by the U.S. Air Force. The Global Hawk is designed for reconnaissance and mapping—it can stay in the air over a battlefield for 36 hours and accurately map thousands of square miles of terrain.

The Boeing E-3 Sentry can provide "real time" data to ground troops and other aircraft. The disk at the rear of the airplane carries an array of powerful radar and imaging equipment.

Escape Maps

During World War II (1939–45), both Allied and Axis aircrew were given specially designed escape maps. With these maps, downed aircrew could find their way to safety.

THE ALLIES' MAPS WERE MADE BY THE MAKERS OF THE GAME Monopoly, using silk, rayon, or tissue paper. The maps were hidden in places such as the heel of a boot or in a cigarette case.

The mapmaking company was also involved in smuggling maps to prisoners of war held in Germany. They hid maps inside Monopoly boards, chess sets, and packs of playing cards, which were sent to prisoner-of-war camps. More than 35,000 American, British, and other Allied prisoners escaped from behind enemy lines, and it is estimated that half of them were carrying a silk map.

Often the prisoners in the camps made maps for themselves to help them escape. Philip Evans and Wallis Heath were both held in a prisoner-of-war camp outside Brunswick, Germany. They set up a printing press using the advice and guidance of other prisoners who

This silk map for British pilots was also first produced in 1943. But in 1953 it was updated for the Cold War. Useful words were provided in Czech and Romanian.

⬆ **Colditz Castle in east Germany. During World War II, Colditz became a well-known prisoner-of-war camp. Between 1941 and 1944, 32 inmates escaped from the castle. With the help of escape maps, about half made it to a safe country.**

were artists, chemists, and carpenters. Copying the silk maps that had been brought inside the camp, they used wall tiles as printing plates and pitch from between the floorboards as the basis for the ink. The men were eventually discovered, but only after they had produced 500 copies of four different maps.

The National Imagery and Mapping Agency in the United States produces maps for use by the armed forces. Among these maps are so-called evasion maps, which are issued to U.S. pilots. In 1995, an Air Force officer named Captain Scott O'Grady was shot down over Bosnia. He managed to avoid being captured by the Serbian forces by using his evasion map. It not only helped him find his way out, but also gave him information about the area he was in and what he could or could not eat. Because it was waterproof, he could use it to keep himself dry, as a groundsheet or tent—and even to carry water or food.

International Maps

The United Nations was established in October 1945 at the end of World War II. Its purpose was to try to preserve peace and avoid any future wars.

ORIGINALLY, THE UN HAD 51 MEMBERS, BUT THAT HAS now increased to 189, nearly all the nations of the world. Today the UN does not just send peacekeeping troops to world troublespots; it has many departments involved in attempting to improve human society in various ways. All these departments use maps, which the UN often creates for itself.

In 1944, in an area of southern Europe known as the Balkans, a new country was created called Yugoslavia. It was formed from Bosnia-Herzegovina, Croatia, Macedonia, Montenegro, Serbia, and Slovenia. Different religious and ethnic groups existed in each of these countries, and for centuries there has been conflict between them.

From 1944 until his death in 1980, Josip Broz Tito ruled the new country of Yugoslavia by force and persuasion. The jealousies and friction that existed between its republics broke out into armed conflicts after 1981.

→ **The Central Intelligence Agency (CIA) has an extensive library of maps of areas where the United States may become involved. This is one of their maps of the area that used to make up the country of Yugoslavia.**

A CIA map of Kosovo. In 1999 a civil war there ended only after intervention by the United States and its allies. After many weeks of bombing, Serbian forces withdrew from Kosovo prior to a NATO invasion from Macedonia.

A world map showing where landmines have been planted in astonishing numbers. Many of them are in countries where the conflict is over, but the countries do not have the financial or technical means to clear them.

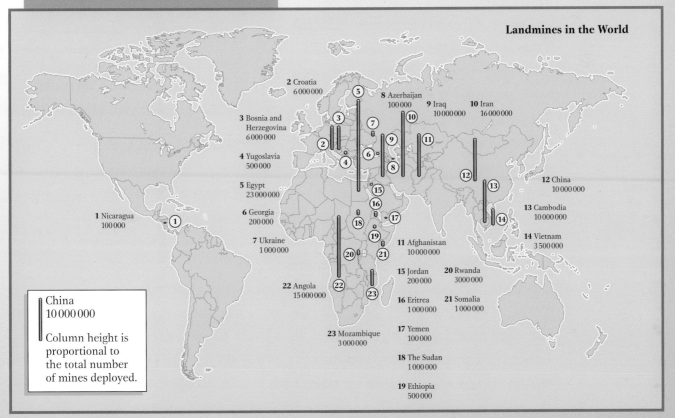

Landmines in the World

1 Nicaragua
100 000

2 Croatia
6 000 000

3 Bosnia and Herzegovina
6 000 000

4 Yugoslavia
500 000

5 Egypt
23 000 000

6 Georgia
200 000

7 Ukraine
1 000 000

8 Azerbaijan
100 000

9 Iraq
10 000 000

10 Iran
16 000 000

11 Afghanistan
10 000 000

12 China
10 000 000

13 Cambodia
10 000 000

14 Vietnam
3 500 000

15 Jordan
200 000

16 Eritrea
1 000 000

17 Yemen
100 000

18 The Sudan
1 000 000

19 Ethiopia
500 000

20 Rwanda
3 000 000

21 Somalia
1 000 000

22 Angola
15 000 000

23 Mozambique
3 000 000

China
10 000 000

Column height is proportional to the total number of mines deployed.

In April 1992, civil war broke out in Bosnia-Herzegovina. The country's two main ethnic groups, Serbs and Bosniaks, were on opposing sides. The Republic of Serbia, aided by the Bosnian-Serbs, tried to take land from Bosnia to make Serbia larger. The Serbs drove any non-Serbian people from parts of Bosnia in a military operation known as "ethnic cleansing." Many non-Serbs who did not flee were killed. A United Nations peacekeeping force was sent to the area, but it struggled to protect the people from Serbian forces.

The headquarters of the United Nations in New York. Founded in the aftermath of a war that killed millions, the United Nations has worked for the last half a century to maintain peace and to improve the lives of people around the world.

Only after NATO air attacks and military defeats by the Bosnian Army did the Serbs agree to peace talks. They took place in Dayton, Ohio. In November 1995, the Dayton Peace Agreement was signed.

An important part of the peace agreement were the maps of the area drawn by the Defense Mapping Agency (it became part of the National Imagery and Mapping Agency in 1996). These maps allowed peace delegates from both sides to see the location of resources and towns in relation to the proposed new borders. Delegates could view a three-dimensional picture of the land they were disputing. Four million dollars worth of high-tech equipment and 55 mapping personnel worked to help in the success of the negotiations.

A similar civil war took place in the Balkans during 1999 in Kosovo. There, as in Bosnia, when the conflicts were settled, the many minefields laid killed many innocent people who were eager to return home. Many millions of mines have been laid throughout the world. Often their location is unknown because no maps were ever drawn. Sometimes the maps are deliberately drawn incorrectly to trick the enemy.

An Umbrella Organization

The UN attempts to work toward improvements in various aspects of life across the globe, such as the defense of human rights, protection for the environment, and the fight against disease and poverty. It does this through more than 30 organizations, including the World Bank; the International Monetary Fund (IMF); the United Nations Educational, Scientific, and Cultural Organization (UNESCO), the United Nations Children's Fund (UNICEF); the International Court of Justice (ICJ); and the World Health Organization (WHO).

In all of its operations the UN sees a great demand for maps. Its own cartographic section produces general maps of more than 100 countries, as well as maps showing where UN peacekeepers are being used. The UN also has a collection of some 80,000 maps, as well as more than 3,000 atlases, gazetteers, travel guides, and cartographic reference works. This library is part of the Dag Hammarskjold Library at the UN Headquarters in New York.

A map made by UN High Commissioner for Refugees in 1999 showing the location of refugee camps in Central Asia. The large number of camps in Pakistan held refugees who had fled from the Taliban regime in Afghanistan.

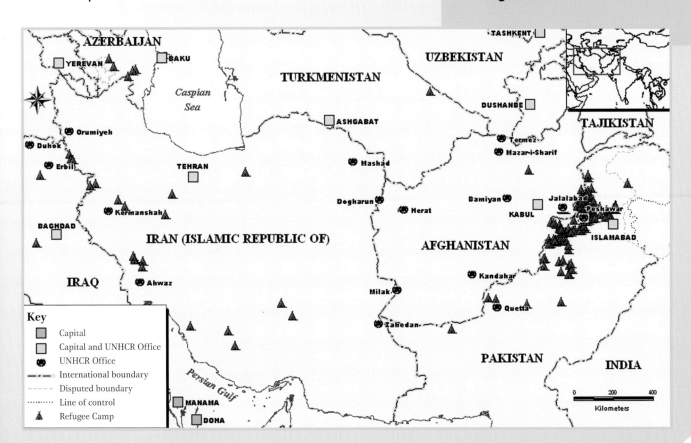

Key
- Capital
- Capital and UNHCR Office
- UNHCR Office
- International boundary
- Disputed boundary
- Line of control
- Refugee Camp

Glossary

Words in *italics* have their own entries in the glossary.

Académie des Sciences (Academy of Sciences) – first established in 1666 as the Académie Royale des Sciences, a small, elite French society in which the most prominent scientific people of the time gathered to advance the progress of science.

aerial photograph (or air photograph) – a photograph looking straight down at Earth

Alexander the Great (356–323 B.C.) – Alexander succeeded his father Philip II as king of Macedonia (an ancient Greek state). Alexander was one of the greatest generals of all time, who conquered much of Asia and the Middle East and influenced the spread of Greek culture.

armament – weapons and equipment used by the military

astronomer – one who studies celestial bodies (planets and stars) and the universe as a whole

atlas – a collection of maps with a uniform design bound together as a book

benchmark – a standard against which something can be measured or assessed

cadastral system – a method of recording ownership of land based on registers, legal documents, and maps showing the boundaries of individual tracts

cartographer – someone who collects information and produces maps from it. The task of making maps is called cartography

An aerial photograph of the crowds gathered for the inauguration of President Barack Obama in January 2009. This picture was taken from an aircraft flying below cloud-level for a better view.

cartouche – originally a cartouche was a list of royal or divine names on an ancient Egyptian scroll. Later, map cartouches were elaborate decorations with dedications inside them, naming the sponsors of the map (often royalty). Today the cartouche often contains the map title, *legend*, and *scale*.

census – a detailed count, usually taken every ten years, of how many people there are in a country, plus details about their lives

Central Powers – during World War I, Germany, Austria-Hungary, and their allies Turkey and Bulgaria

Churchill, Sir Winston (1874–1965) – prime minister who led Britain during World War II from 1940 to 1945; a statesman, soldier, and author

Cold War – the relationship that existed between the U.S. (and its allies) and the former USSR (and its allies) from the end of World War II to about 1990. Both groups kept large numbers of troops and weapons in the event of the other side attacking them.

colony – a group of people who settle in a land distant from their homeland but retain close economic and cultural links with it; the territory they inhabit and control

comprehensive – including everything, so as to be complete

coordinates – the pair of values that define a position on a graph or on a map with a coordinate system (such as latitude and longitude). On a map the coordinates "55°N 45°E" indicate a position of 55 degrees north of latitude, 45 degrees east of longitude.

cruise missile – an unmanned rocket that, when launched from a ship or submarine, can navigate to its target by skimming low over the surface, avoiding enemy radar and

matching the picture of the ground with the preprogrammed map of the route to the eventual target

Cuban missile crisis – in 1962, the USSR began shipping nuclear missiles into Cuba. Once U-2 spy planes had spotted the missiles, the U.S. blockaded the island to stop the missile shipments. After a tense week with both sides preparing for war, the Soviet premier Nikita Khrushchev withdrew the missiles.

democracy – a form of government in which all of the adult people in a country have the right to vote in elections to decide who is to govern them

detonate – to explode or make something explode

engraving – the art of inscribing a design onto a block, plate, or other surface used for printing

espionage – the use of spying or spies to gather secret information

ethnic cleansing – the removal of people of a different color, religion, or ethnic background from that of the dominant group of an area through force or intimidation and sometimes murder

gazetteer – a list of names of places, with their location specified; often accompanied by a map

geological maps – maps that show the structure of the rocks underneath an area

geology – the study of the rocks under Earth's surface and their structure

geospatial information – information about where things are on Earth's surface and what their characteristics are

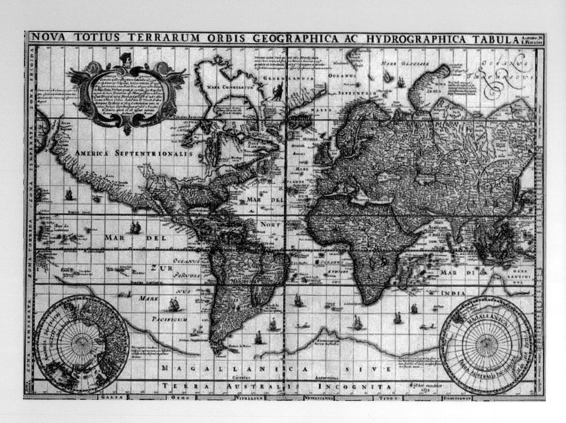

gerrymandering – the process of manipulating voting districts in order to distort the results of elections

Global Positioning System (GPS) – a system of 24 man-made satellites orbiting Earth and sending out highly accurate radio signals indicating where they are. A GPS receiver held by someone on Earth can interpret the signals and calculate the receiver's position on Earth.

grid system – a reference system that uses a mesh of horizontal and vertical lines over the face of a map to pinpoint the position of places. The mesh of lines often helps show distance of locations east and north from a set position. The zero point can be any convenient location and is often the bottom-left corner of the map.

infrastructure – the public facilities built up over a number of years that are used by people in their daily lives. Examples include the transportation system, power supply, and sewerage system.

The Mercator projection was an important advance in the science of cartography. It allowed the curved surface of Earth to be represented as a two-dimensional image without distorting the lines of latitude and longitude. This made it ideal for navigators.

Internet – the network of interconnected computers throughout the world linked by wires and satellites and running software to allow them to communicate with each other

land mines – explosive devices usually buried just under the surface of the ground and sensitive to humans walking or driving over them. They are used to target enemy soldiers, but after military action has finished, they are a major danger to civilians.

legend – a list of all the symbols used on a map with an explanation of their meaning

munitions – military supplies such as weapons and ammunition

National Imagery and Mapping Agency (NIMA) – an organization that produces maps and other geographic information for the American military

national mapping agency – a government-run organization responsible for producing mainly *topographic maps* of an entire country

Nazi – member of the National Socialist German Worker's Party that seized control of Germany in 1933 under Adolf Hitler

North Atlantic Treaty Organization (NATO) – a group of countries in Europe and North America that have agreed to work together to defend themselves in the event of one or more of them being attacked

Ordnance Survey – the national mapping agency of Great Britain

pesticide – a chemical substance used to kill pests, especially insects

phenomena – a fact or occurrence, ordinary or extraordinary, that can be observed

photogrammetry – the science of making accurate measurements from photographs of the world

plate tectonics – the study of the movements of the plates or sections that make up Earth's crust. These plates ride on the semimolten rock inside the crust.

propaganda – a way of altering the attitudes, opinions, and views of another person about an issue by producing written documents or graphical materials such as maps or through the spoken word

quarries – an open excavation from which stone or other material is extracted by blasting, cutting, or drilling

radar – a method of detecting distant objects by bouncing high-frequency radio waves off them and interpreting the return signal

reconnaissance – for the military, the task of obtaining information about the land and the enemy's position

relief – the shape of Earth's surface, especially its hills, mountains, and depressions

San Andreas Fault – a major fault in Earth's crust in Southern California, where earthquake risk is high. The disastrous San Francisco earthquake of 1906 was caused by movement along the fault (see *also* plate tectonics).

The task of mapping and removing the world's minefields is huge and daunting. Some countries are still working to clear land mines buried during World War II.

Land surveying is vital for the creation of accurate maps. The process is still usually performed by surveyors using instruments such as theodolites.

scale – the ratio of the size of a map to the area of the real world that it represents

seismic survey – using explosives to set off small earth tremors. Interpretation of the results reveals information about the structure of the rocks beneath.

surveying – the measuring of altitudes, angles, and distances on the land surface in order to obtain accurate positions of features that can be mapped. Surveying the oceans and seas also means measuring distances and angles between visible coastal positions, but the third dimension measured is depth rather than height.

tactical – planning to or supporting military operations

terrain – a geographic area; the physical features of an area of land

theodolite – a surveying instrument used to figure out the angle between two points on Earth's surface viewed from a third point

topographic map – a map that shows natural features such as hills, rivers, and forests, and man-made features such as roads and buildings

triangulation – a surveying method, using angles alone to figure out the position of points on Earth's surface

United Nations – an organization set up in October 1945 at the end of World War II in order to try to preserve peace and avoid future wars. Almost every country in the world now belongs to the UN.

United States Geological Survey – the national mapping agency of the U.S. It also undertakes scientific work in other fields such as geology and environmental sciences.

West Nile Virus – an illness marked by fever, headache, muscle ache, and skin rash that is spread chiefly by mosquitoes

Further Reading and Web Sites

Aczel, Amir D. *The Riddle of the Compass: The Invention That Changed the World*. New York: Harcourt, 2001.

Arnold, Caroline. *The Geography Book: Activities for Exploring, Mapping, and Enjoying Your World*. New York: Wiley, 2002.

Barber, Peter, and April Carlucci, eds. *The Lie of the Land*. London: British Library Publications, 2001.

Brown, Carron, ed. *The Best-Ever Book of Exploration*. New York: Kingfisher Books, 2002.

Davis, Graham. *Make Your Own Maps*. New York: Sterling, 2008.

Deboo, Ana. *Mapping the Seas and Skies*. Chicago: Heinemann-Raintree, 2007.

Dickinson, Rachel. *Tools of Navigation: A Kid's Guide to the History & Science of Finding Your Way*. White River Junction, VT: Nomad Press, 2005.

Doak, Robin S. *Christopher Columbus: Explorer of the New World*. Minneapolis, MN: Compass Point Books, 2005.

Ehrenberg, Ralph E. *Mapping the World: An Illustrated History of Cartography*. Washington, D.C.: National Geographic, 2005.

Field, Paula, ed. *The Kingfisher Student Atlas of North America*. Boston: Kingfisher, 2005.

Ganeri, Anita, and Andrea Mills. *Atlas of Exploration*. New York: DK Publishing, 2008.

Graham, Alma, ed. *Discovering Maps*. Maplewood, NJ: Hammond World Atlas Corporation, 2004.

Harvey, Miles. *The Island of Lost Maps: A True Story of Cartographic Crime*. New York: Random House, 2000.

Harwood, Jeremy. *To the Ends of the Earth: 100 Maps That Changed the World*. Newton Abbot, United Kingdom: David and Charles, 2006.

Haywood, John. *Atlas of World History*. New York: Barnes and Noble, 1997.

Hazen, Walter A. *Everyday Life: Exploration & Discovery*. Tuscon, AZ: Good Year Books, 2005.

Henzel, Cynthia Kennedy. *Mapping History*. Edina, MN: Abdo Publishing, 2008.

Jacobs, Frank. *Strange Maps: An Atlas of Cartographic Curiosities*. New York: Viking Studio, 2009.

Keay, John. *The Great Arc: The Dramatic Tale of How India Was Mapped and Everest Was Named*. New York: HarperCollins, 2000.

Levy, Janey. *Mapping America's Westward Expansion: Applying Geographic Tools And Interpreting Maps*. New York: Rosen Publishing, 2005.

Levy, Janey. *The Silk Road: Using a Map Scale to Measure Distances*. New York: PowerKids Press, 2005.

McDonnell, Mark D. *Maps on File*. New York: Facts on File, 2007.

McNeese, Tim. *Christopher Columbus and the Discovery of the Americas*. Philadelphia: Chelsea House, 2006.

Mitchell, Robert, and Donald Prickel. *Contemporary's Number Power: Graphs, Tables, Schedules, and Maps*. Lincolnwood, IL: Contemporary Books, 2000.

Oleksy, Walter G. *Mapping the Seas*. New York: Franklin Watts, 2003.

Oleksy, Walter G. *Mapping the Skies*. New York: Franklin Watts, 2003.

Resnick, Abraham. *Maps Tell Stories Too: Geographic Connections to American History*. Bloomington, IN: IUniverse, 2002.

Rirdan, Daniel. *Wide Ranging World Map*. Phoenix, AZ: Exploration, 2002.

Ross, Val. *The Road to There: Mapmakers and Their Stories*. Toronto, Canada: Tundra Books, 2009.

Rumsey, David, and Edith M. Punt. *Cartographica Extraordinaire: The Historical Map Transformed.* Redlands, CA: Esri Press, 2004.

Short, Charles Rennie. *The World through Maps.* Buffalo, NY: Firefly Books, 2003.

Smith, A. G. *Where Am I? The Story of Maps and Navigation.* Toronto, Canada: Fitzhenry and Whiteside, 2001.

Taylor, Barbara. *Looking at Maps.* North Mankato, MN: Franklin Watts, 2007.

Taylor, Barbara. *Maps and Mapping.* New York: Kingfisher, 2002.

Virga, Vincent. *Cartographia: Mapping Civilizations.* London: Little, Brown and Company, 2007.

Wilkinson, Philip. *The World of Exploration.* New York: Kingfisher, 2006.

Wilson, Patrick. *Navigation and Signalling.* Broomall, PA: Mason Crest Publishers, 2002.

Winchester, Simon. *The Map That Changed the World: William Smith and the Birth of Modern Geology.* New York: HarperCollins, 2001.

Zuravicky, Orli. *Map Math: Learning About Latitude and Longitude Using Coordinate Systems.* New York: PowerKids Press, 2005.

Online Resources

www.davidrumsey.com
The David Rumsey map collection. This online library contains around 20,000 historical and modern maps.

http://dma.jrc.it
The mapping collection of the European Commission Joint Research Center. Includes ineractive maps as well as maps documenting environmental and human disasters around the world.

http://etc.usf.edu/Maps/
The University of South Florida's online mapping library. The collection includes historical and modern maps from around the world.

www.lib.utexas.edu/maps
The University of Texas's online map library. The collection includes old CIA maps, historical maps, and thematic maps from around the world.

www2.lib.virginia.edu/exhibits/lewis_clark
An online exhibition at the University of Virginia with information on historic expeditions, including Lewis and Clark.

http://maps.google.com
Google's online mapping resource, includes conventional maps and satellite images for most of the world, as well as street-level photography of Western urban centers.

http://maps.nationalgeographic.com
National Geographic's online mapping service.

http://memory.loc.gov/ammem/gmdhtml/
Map collections from 1500–1999 at the Library of Congress. The collection includes maps made by early explorers, maps of military campaigns, and thematic maps on a variety of topics.

www.nationalatlas.gov
Online national atlas for the United States. Includes customizable topographic maps on a range of different themes.

http://strangemaps.wordpress.com
A frequently updated collection of unusual maps, from maps of imaginary lands to creative ways of displaying data in map form.

www.unc.edu/awmc/mapsforstudents.html
A large collection of free maps, covering many different subjects and regions, hosted by the University of North Carolina.

www.un.org/Depts/Cartographic/
  english/htmain.htm
United Nations mapping agency website. contains maps of the world from 1945 to the present day, including UN maps of conflict areas and disputed territories.

Index

Page numbers written in **boldface** refer to pictures or captions.